**U.S. Fish & Wildlife Service**

# National Fish Passage Program

*Creating Aquatic Possibilities*

*FY2012 Annual Report and Future Outlook*

PENOBSCOT RIVER
RESTORATION PROJECT

# From the Director

Rivers are the lifeblood of our nation, and always have been. The course of our rivers has long shaped where we live and work. And we've come to realize that the health of rivers and the communities they support is linked to their ability to flow.

Free-flowing rivers are vital to our nation's aquatic species. Native fish, shellfish, amphibians, waterfowl and plants depend on the ebb and flow of rivers at many stages of their lives. And free-flowing rivers do so much more; they help with flood control, provide recreational opportunities and are a source of inspiration.

It's estimated that 74,000 dams dot the American landscape, thousands of which are small, aging and no longer serve a purpose.

These derelict structures impede the passage of native fish, destroy spawning habitat and degrade water quality by preventing stream flow that flushes our river systems. The dams also reduce river-based recreational and economic opportunities for local communities. And in some cases, aging dams threaten to flood downstream communities should they fail, or otherwise endanger human safety.

So I'm pleased to report that the U.S. Fish and Wildlife Service and its partners reopened more than 2,500 miles of streams and 36,000 associated wetland acres to fish passage in 2012, making it one of our most successful years for restoration.

One of the biggest projects by the Service's National Fish Passage Program was the removal of the Great Works Dam on Maine's Penobscot River. The removal of the dam marked the beginning of what will be largest river restoration project in the country. It will make more than 1,000 miles of native

habitat available for federally listed Atlantic salmon and other aquatic species for the public to enjoy. It will restore a cultural and natural resource for the Penobscot Indian Nation, which is linked to the Penobscot River.

The National Fish Passage Program also improves fish passage through road-crossing structures, such as culverts and channel-spanning bridges. Tropical Storm Irene has taught us a great deal about helping New England communities recover and withstand future floods through the science of fish passage.

In September 2012, rains drenched Alaska, resulting in a federal flood disaster. Yet 99 percent of road-stream crossings that had been retrofitted with larger, fish-friendly channel-spanning structures survived the flooding, saving hundreds of thousands of dollars in recovery costs. Commerce and transportation continued uninterrupted despite the disaster – and we protected important aquatic species.

In the coming year, the Service will continue working with partners to wisely rebuild communities after Superstorm Sandy. With new and existing partners, we hope in 2013 to restore more than 300 river miles and 15,000 wetland acres across the country and expand our reach to communities across the nation including the agricultural community.

Unfortunately, some of this work may not be accomplished due to the impacts of federal budget sequestration. We hope to keep fish passage as a national priority. Restoring free-flowing streams wherever possible will help fish and other aquatic species, with the American public as the real beneficiary.

---

To obtain a copy of this report, please contact Susan Wells - National Fish Passage Program Coordinator at: susan_wells@fws.gov.

Report produced for the Fish and Aquatic Conservation - National Fish Passage Program by José Barrios.

**On the Cover:**
*Blessing by the Penobscot Indian Nation prior to the demolition of the Great Works Dam in Maine in June of 2012.*

Photo Credit: USFWS

# Chief's Corner

America's rivers and streams form the network of aquatic corridors that are the backbone of many of our nation's ecosystems and economies. As these systems go, so goes the viability of hundreds of aquatic species, as well as the communities that depend upon healthy waterways as a way of life.

The Fish and Wildlife Service is proud to partner with agencies and organizations from coast-to-coast to restore aquatic connectivity, and to support healthy, functioning natural resources and the ecological and recreational benefits that they provide.

Tom Busiahn / USFWS

*Mike Weimer, Division Chief - Fish and Aquatic Conservation, Washington, DC.*

# National Fish Passage Program
## *Creating Aquatic Possibilities*

*FY2012 Fish Passage Report: This National Fish Passage Program Annual Report provides account-ability of our activities to our constituents, the American people, on what we have accomplished with appropriated funding in fiscal year 2012 (October 1, 2011- September 31, 2012). This report highlights the important work the U.S. Fish & Wildlife Service, has completed in concert with our partners across the country to implement the program.*

## About the program

The National Fish Passage Program (NFPP) provides funding and technical assistance in all 50 States to recon-nect aquatic habitat by eliminating or bypassing barriers. Fisheries science demonstrates that in-river movement is the key to survival and sustainability for these animals. Addressing the decline of aquatic species populations was the motivation for the creation of the voluntary, non-regulatory Fish Passage Program in 1999. Housed within the Fish and Aquatic Conservation and administered in the field by Fish and Wildlife Conservation Offices (FWCO), a national network of U.S. Fish & Wildlife Service (USFWS) biologists and fish passage engineers has been created to follow the Service's Strategic Habitat Conservation (SHC) model when implementing fish passage. Following the SHC model means the NFPP identifies, prioritizes, funds, plans, designs, reviews, inspects, monitors, and evaluates projects, to remove obsolete dams, replace impassable culverts, build bypasses, construct low-water crossings, and install fish-ways and fish screens in cooperation with State and Federal agencies, non-governmental organizations, universities, and individuals. The NFPP has a strong track record recon-necting our nation's rivers. The NFPP has removed over a 1,000 barriers, restoring more than 20,000 miles of stream access and 155,000 acres of wetlands. These efforts are the first steps in addressing the more than six million remain-ing fish passage barriers across the country. Many of these barriers, once the drivers of the industrial revolution, are now abandoned, obsolete, and unsafe to swimmers, boaters, and flood-prone communities downstream. They repre-sent costly burdens to small towns and individuals and they threaten aquatic species survival as well as human safety. The NFPP is working to address these challenges across the country.

> *"The National Fish Passage Program (NFPP) has been instru-mental in the removal of fish passage barriers in the White River Watershed in Oceana County, Michigan. In 2012, funds received from US Fish & Wildlife Service's NFPP, enabled us to replace two additional stream crossings, bringing our total to six. This program has given the Oceana County Road Commission the opportunity to replace failing infrastructure with more durable and safer timber bridges that otherwise may not have been possible."*
>
> -Oceana County Road Commission, Michigan

# National Fish Passage Program Achievements

## 2012 Program Highlights

Since 1999, the NFPP has been working to achieve successful biological and socio-economic outcomes:

- $11 billion in economic value to local communities.
- Removed 1,345 fish passage barriers.
- Reopened access to 20,229 stream miles.
- Reconnected 155,454 acres of wetlands.
- Benefited over 90 species of fish and freshwater mussels.
- $79 million invested in projects, engineering and administration.
- 70% of the funds applied on-the-ground.
- 3:1 ratio of non-federal match to NFPP funding.
- Over 750 project partners.
- Projects supported 219,195 jobs.

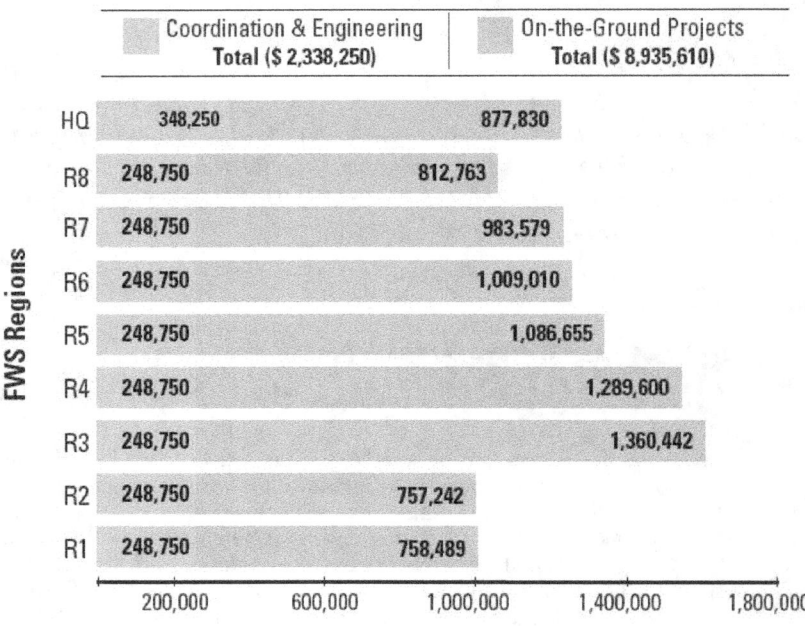

**2012 Funding Allocations**

Coordination & Engineering Total ($ 2,338,250) | On-the-Ground Projects Total ($ 8,935,610)

| FWS Regions | Coordination & Engineering | On-the-Ground Projects |
|---|---|---|
| HQ | 348,250 | 877,830 |
| R8 | 248,750 | 812,763 |
| R7 | 248,750 | 983,579 |
| R6 | 248,750 | 1,009,010 |
| R5 | 248,750 | 1,086,655 |
| R4 | 248,750 | 1,289,600 |
| R3 | 248,750 | 1,360,442 |
| R2 | 248,750 | 757,242 |
| R1 | 248,750 | 758,489 |

Allocated Funding ($)

---

*Note: Please refer to page 35 for a map with FWS administrative regions and regional office locations.*

## 2012 Accomplishments

Regional breakdown of National Fish Passage Program projects completed in Fiscal Year 2012:

| Regions | Barriers removed or bypassed | Miles opened to fish passage | Acres opened to fish passage | Barrier inventories |
|---|---|---|---|---|
| 1 | 23 | 252 | 253 | 0 |
| 2 | 2 | 14 | 148 | 0 |
| 3 | 19 | 838 | 330 | 2 |
| 4 | 14 | 63 | 35,564 | 0 |
| 5* | 127 | 924 | 300 | 27 |
| 6 | 19 | 345 | 0 | 0 |
| 7 | 15 | 26 | 35 | 0 |
| 8 | 7 | 59 | 0 | 4 |
| HQ | 1 | 25 | 0 | 0 |
| TOTALS | 227 | 2,546 | 36,630 | 33 |

In fiscal year 2012 (October 1, 2011 – September 31, 2012) projects were completed in over 40 States with 300 partners across the Nation. These included fish passage barrier removals, engineering, planning and partnership coordination, monitoring and evaluation, and barrier inventories to support the Geospatial Fisheries Information Network (GeoFIN).

\* Totals combined with regional fish passage engineering work.

# What We Accomplished in 2012

## Increasing Awareness – Getting Our Story Out

- Presented the White River Partnership with $100,000 for Tropical Storm Irene response.

- Briefed legislative staff, met with TU, USFS, FEMA, and participated in a NFPP briefing with the USFWS Director, regarding Tropical Storm Irene flooding recovery efforts in VT.

- Communicated with Service field staff on briefing local Congressional offices on NFPP. Subsequently, field staff visited District Offices.

- Conducted Congressional briefings in Washington, DC on the NFPP; also met with FS, TU and FishNet.

- Produced three videos on fish passage in the Northeast United States and one national fish passage video.

- Provided a field tour for Rebecca Wodder, Senior Advisor to the Secretary of the Interior, visiting four hurricane-related fish passage projects in Becket and Chester, MA. Tour included representatives from TNC, TU, State of MA, Westfield River Watershed Association, and NRCS.

- The NFPP Coordinator toured the VT Tropical Storm Irene projects and met with the White River Partnership and FEMA. FEMA videoed an interview with the National NFPP Coordinator talking about flood resiliency and the collaboration between FWS and FEMA.

> 'The County of Ventura completed a barrier removal project in March 2012 replacing a dry weather crossing with a bridge over San Antonio Creek near Casitas Springs California. A portion of the project focused on fish passage and habitat improvement actions on County property. This effort was accomplished in partnership with the Fish and Wildlife Service's Local Coastal Program utilizing funding from the Service's National Fish Passage Program (NFPP). The FWS NFPP funds and Coastal Program assistance were instrumental in the project's success.'
>
> **-Theresa Lubin, Ventura County Parks Manager**

## Enhancing Professional and Technical Capacity

- Surveyed Fisheries field staff technical capacity in fish passage and implemented pilot training to include the Rosgen Stream Restoration courses, Forest Service Stream Simulation, and hands-on project training with fish passage mentors in Fisheries and Ecological Services (ES) program as foundation-level training.

- Sponsored and exhibited at the second annual 2012 National Fish Passage Conference in Amherst, MA.

- Initiated collaboration with National Wildlife Refuge System MAT Team and National Fish Hatchery heavy equipment operators in conjunction with ES field staff to do on-the-ground implementation of fish passage projects.

- Worked with Forest Service and NGO's to draft article on the flood resiliency of fish passage culverts for the American Fisheries Society transactions, to be published in 2013.

- Hired University of Massachusetts Fish Passage and Ecohydrology degree graduate as the program's next fish passage engineer.

## Increasing Program Resources and Outcomes

- February 2012 - $1.5 million increase in the President's proposed budget for FY 2012 translated into a $500,000 increase in the Continuing Resolution for the NFPP.

- Identified and worked with local communities to implement seven America's Great Outdoors projects.

- Convened a group of Federal agencies and NGOs in a summit in Washington, DC to discuss response and concerns identified post-Tropical Storm Irene recovery efforts.

- With FWS Region 5, organized event with the Secretary of the Interior to celebrate removal of the Great Works Dam on the Penobscot River in cooperation with the Penobscot River Restoration Trust.

# RIVERS The Life Blood of America

Take Me Fishing image library / RBFF

## *America's Great Outdoors*

The America's Great Outdoors initiative encourages federal agencies to listen to their partners and the American people regarding ways to reconnect the public with the nation's richest natural resources—the great outdoors. In early 2012, Secretary of the Interior Salazar took this idea even further by recognizing rivers as the life blood of America intimately linked to the health of the habitats, critters, and our communities. The Rivers Initiative identified projects in all 50 states of which the National Fish Passage Program played a leading role in numerous projects including the Harpeth Dam removal in Tennessee, the Penobscot River restoration project in Maine, the fish passage education project on the Milwaukee River in Wisconsin, and the Gimlet Creek crossing in South Dakota that restored fish passage in the creek as well as provide wise use for all terrain vehicles. Restoring fish passage is about more than just helping aquatic species, it benefits communities by enhancing the resource, providing healthy functioning river systems, reducing catastrophic impacts, and increases opportunities for the American people to get outside to fish, paddle, watch wildlife, and to enjoy all the wonders of free-flowing water and America's Great Outdoors.

USFWS

# Penobscot River
## A Milestone for River Conservation

The Penobscot River Restoration project, an America's Great Outdoors project, is sure to be one of the largest landscape scale restoration projects in the country once completed. The Penobscot River is the second largest watershed in Maine draining more than 8,500 square miles. Historically the river was home to 11 species of sea run fish including Atlantic salmon and Atlantic sturgeon supplying consistent subsistence fishing for the Penobscot Indian Nation and numerous local economic benefits.

Early in the 19th century industry harnessed the river for logging and power supply. Such activities polluted the river. The dams built for power soon became hazards and inhibited movement of the sea-run fish causing eventual listing under the Endangered Species Act.

The identity of the Penobscot Indian Nation is intimately connected to the river and has taken a toll on their traditions and culture. They have been unable to exercise their fishing rights for the past 100 years because of the decline in sea- run fish populations.

With the removal of the Great Works Dam, the Penobscot River and its communities are beginning to revitalize. In June 2012, then Secretary of the Interior Ken Salazar, leaders from the business communities, local communities, conservation organizations, and local, state and federal governments came together to celebrate. The first dam in a series of three that will be removed or bypassed was being demolished. Once complete, more than 1,000 river miles will be reconnected to the Atlantic Ocean opening up opportunities for fishing, paddling, wildlife viewing, and numerous other activities that have not been possible for more than a century. This restoration is occurring while maintaining the same level of power generation, proving that aquatic habitat conservation does not mean a community cannot have both a vital power supply and a vibrant natural resource. This only helps to increase a communities vitality and economic richness.

*Former Secretary of the Interior, Ken Salazar.*

*Blessing by the Penobscot Indian Nation prior to the demolition of the Great Works Dam.*

*Demolition of the Great Works dam is the start of an effort to open nearly 1,000 miles of habitat to 11 species of fish that haven't had open access to the Penobscot river for two centuries.*

# National Fish Passage Program Awards

## 2012 Partner of the Year Award

The White River Partnership's Greg Russ, project manager, and Mary Russ, executive director, accepted the NFPP National Partner of the Year Award at their annual meeting in Rochester, VT. The Partnership launched a rapid response to the devasting Tropical Storm Irene in 2011, ensuring both additional funding, engineering and technical assistance to repair road crossings in the upper White River watershed. Their subsequent advocacy for fish-friendly culverts helped spur a national discussion on road crossing standards.

*Truckee Meadows Water Authority (TMWA) is indeed grateful for the support from the National Fish Passage Program (NFPP) and Lahontan Fish Hatchery Complex during the pre and post project monitoring. Through NFPP funding support, TMWA was able to purchase and successfully monitor fish movement using state-of-the-art hydro acoustic tags and receivers. Use of this technology was successful as data collected from the tagging and monitoring effort indicated definite fish passage improvement upon completion of the new water intake project.*

**-Ron Penrose, M.S., P.E. Project Manager; Truckee Meadows Water Authority, Reno, NV.**

## Biologist Award

Mr. Stewart Cogswell (left) is a Fish Biologist at the Green Bay FWCO. He has been part of the fisheries conservation community in the Great Lakes Region since 1991. His efforts have included removing and bypassing many impediments to fish passage, working to identify and assess existing barriers, hosting training opportunities and workshops, and playing an active role on our Region 3 Habitat Team. Mr. Cogswell was honored by the NFPP (Brian Elkington, Regional Fish Passage Coordinator-right) "Fish Passage Biologist of the Year" for his efforts to promote fish passage, create and build partnerships to further our work, and think creatively to provide further fish passage opportunities.

# Tropical Storm Irene
## *Rapid Cross Program Response*

USFWS

USFWS

*Temporary culvert used to open road post Irene.*

Soon after Tropical Storm Irene blew through the Northeast in 2011, a few things became apparent: (1) local communities suffered untold damage and loss of important road infrastructure at stream crossings; (2) culverts survived the 100 to 500-year flood event if fish-friendly sizing and positioning informed the previous replacements; and, (3) existing response capacity of any single group or agency (funding and technical support) was inadequate during and immediately after the emergency.

The NFPP focused response on restoring fish passage in Vermont but also provided additional funding and technical support for projects in New York, Massachusetts and Pennsylvania. Moreover, past and subsequent experiences in Minnesota, South and North Dakota, and Alaska parallel the findings in Vermont. For example, in Alaska, 79 out of 81 fish-

friendly projects in the Matanuska-Susitna Borough survived a 100-year flood in Fall 2012.

In 2012, a consortium of state and federal agencies and NGOs convened in Washington, DC to review lessons learned and to develop recommendations for improved response in the future. Recommendations included establishing and implementing consistent road crossing standards that yield unrestricted rivers within and beyond state boundaries, cross-program and cross-agency strike teams for emergency engineering and technical response in

support of state needs, complete surveys to identify existing potential for failures and provide education, information and guidance targeting states, towns, department of transportation, and commercial heavy equipment operators increase on-the-ground knowledge and capacity for successful fish passage and stream restoration.

USFWS

*Replacement bridge for temporary damaged culvert.*

USFWS

*Project completed.*

# Flood Proof
## *Engineering Solutions*

### *Fish-Friendly Culverts Hold Tight through 100-year flood*

Matanuska-Susitna Borough, located in South-central Alaska, was approved for FEMA Federal Disaster relief funds to help respond to extensive flood damage sustained in September 2012. Many roads with undersized culverts or located near rivers were overtopped by flood waters, resulting in extensive damage, repair costs, and road closures. However, the 81 road-stream crossings retrofitted with larger, fish friendly channel-spanning structures over the past 10 years survived the flooding with flying colors. These improvements are the result of investments of funding and USFWS staff time into partnerships and projects that restore fish passage.

This 100-year flood event showed that road-stream crossing structures designed to pass juvenile fish and retain

natural stream function are also immensely valuable from a road maintenance and public safety perspective. Jim Jenson (Matanuska-Susitna Borough Director of Operations and Maintenance) explained, "the fish passage culverts definitely lowered the potential for failure on many roads during these last floods." Sixty-five percent of inventoried culverts in the Mat-Su Borough Valley still present partial or total barriers for fish seeking upstream or downstream passage. Culverts that don't pass fish oftentimes don't pass floods either. Installing fish-friendly road-stream crossing structures can help sustain healthy fish populations, improve public safety, and improve stream flows no matter what the weather.

*An undersized culvert on Nurses Creek sustained damage at the inlet and outlet and caused flood waters to overtop the road.* Katrina Mueller / USFWS

Post-flood: the Mat-Su Borough and USFWS up-graded a 5 foot round culvert on Colter Creek with this fish-friendly 14 foot arch following 2006 floods. Fish-friendly culverts have water depths, velocities, and channel characteristics that mimic the natural stream.

William Rice / USFWS

# Building Fish Passage Capacity

## Enhancing Professional and Technical Capacity

*Hatchery and fishery management biologists and engineers received training in fish passage and stream restoration to better meet the needs of the Fishery Program in the future. Skills were developed using the Rosgen methodology as well as U.S. Forest Service stream simulation. Hands-on cross program experience was provided during the Vermont flood response, Clifford Dam removal (MD), and remnant log drive dam removal (ME).*

## New Fish Passage Engineer

Jesus Morales is the latest addition to the fish passage team, joining the Northeast Region Fisheries Program in 2012. Born and raised in the island of Puerto Rico, Jesus earned his B.S. degree in Civil Engineering from the University of Puerto Rico, Mayagüez. He then went on to pursue his Master of Science in Civil Engineering with a specialization in Fish Passage Engineering, from the Civil & Environmental Engineering Department at the University of  Massachusetts - Amherst. Mr. Morales specializes in stream restoration projects, hydrological analyses, geomorphological studies, and hydraulics for fish passage.

*2012 Anchorage Alaska Fish Passage Workshop: participants working through culvert design exercises.*

# Teamwork: The Key for Success

William Rice / USFWS

Katrina Mueller / USFWS

## 2012 Anchorage Fish Passage Workshops

Engineering and hydrological solutions to fish passage problems in Alaska are presented annually at a series of free workshops co-organized by USFWS and Alaska Department of Fish and Game. The two days workshops have a classroom and field component - providing state-of-the-art information about the design and construction of embedded culverts that simulate stream conditions and maximize fish passage. Since 2006, over 350 consultants, permitters, planners, project managers, biologists, resource managers, and engineers representing state, federal, municipal, and tribal agency staff, NGOs, and private firms have participated in the Alaska fish passage workshops.

*Following two days in the classroom, 2012 Kodiak Fish Passage Workshop participants visited and discussed a broad spectrum of road-stream crossings with Alaska (R7) FWS fish passage engineer, Bill Rice.*

# Working Lands & Water

Humans have diverted water from natural sources for agricultural, industrial, municipal and various other uses for thousands of years. In doing so, they also divert fish. A wide range of screening technologies have been developed and employed to ensure safe fish passage at diversions; however, many remain unscreened throughout the western United States. The NFPP and partners recognize that water diversions are crucial to people, but also provide opportunities to protect native fish populations by ensuring that fish are not diverted.

The U.S. Fish and Wildlife Service's NFPP is working to develop and implement effective fish and debris screening technology and implement practices to protect fish, aquatic habitat and the ability of Americans to continue to efficiently utilize water. Specifically, NFPP funds have been used to create solutions at small diversion sites in streams or at headwaters of larger river systems. These sites have routinely been overlooked during large-scale fish screening efforts due to the small volumes of water they divert. Still these smaller diversion sites can be highly detrimental to juvenile fish and are a vital source of water to smaller agricultural operations and municipalities.

It is important to recognize that much of the infrastructure associated with these diversion sites is aging and was built using less efficient methods. By focusing on smaller diversion sites, NFPP is often the only funding vehicle through which smaller diverters may be able to protect and upgrade their diversion sites. Dan Kominek, a diversion operator in the Klamath Basin of Northern California and Southern Oregon and recipient of NFPP funding in 2011 summed it up by stating, "the funding we received from NFPP allowed us to remove a barrier to fish passage and install a fish screen on our irrigation diversion. Additionally, the resulting irrigation system will make water savings possible as well as greatly enhance our labor efficiencies."

*Fish Ladder: Although the preferred restoration action for fish passage is the complete removal of the barrier, this is often not feasible. Fish ladders (or fishway) are a practical alternative for providing upstream passage to migratory fish and other aquatic organisms especially at diversion dams.*

USFWS

*Ray irrigation diversion and dam before.*

*Restoring fish passage at Ray diversion opened 14 miles to native Yellowstone cutthroat trout*

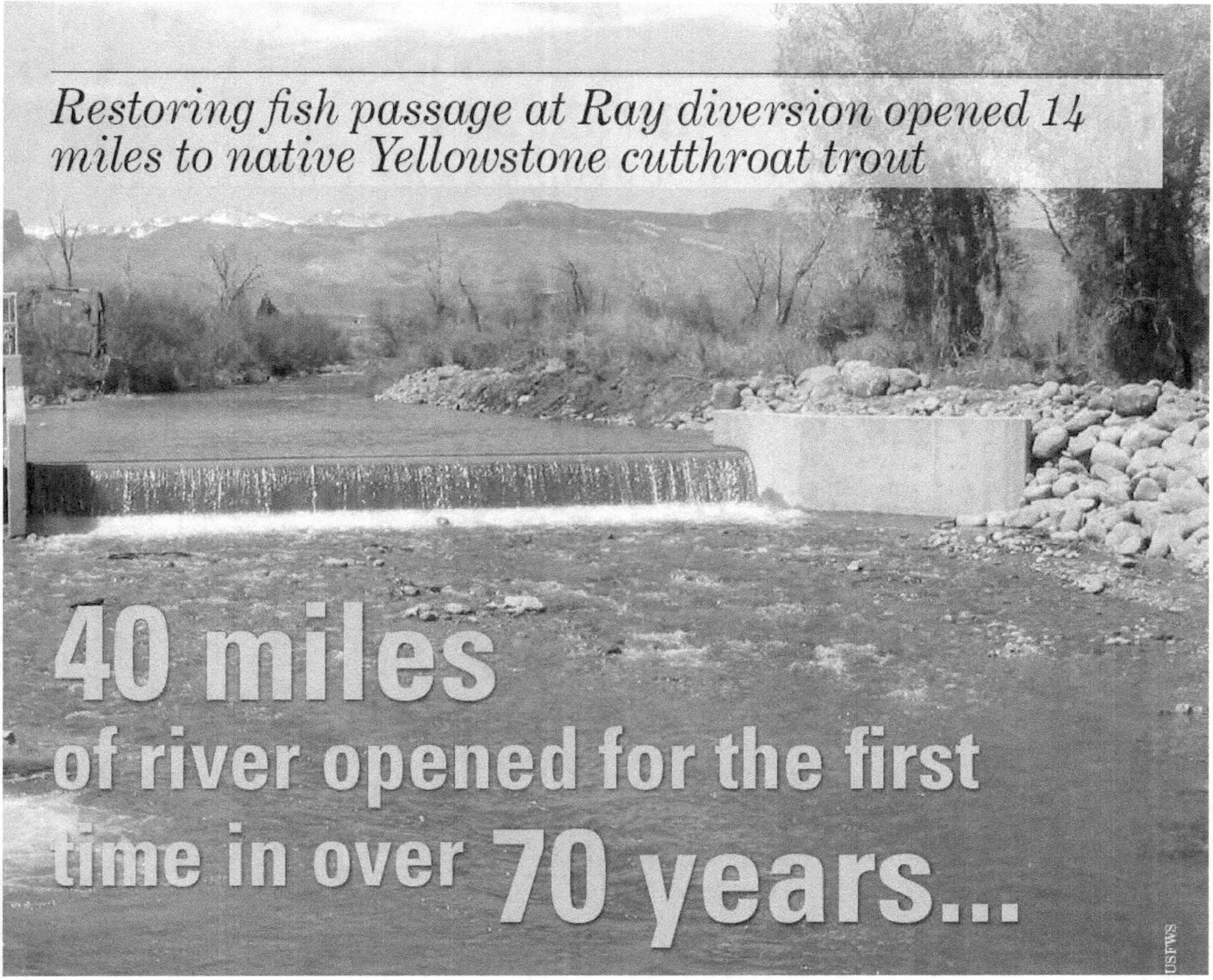

**40 miles** of river opened for the first time in over **70 years...**

USFWS

USFWS

*Fish Screens in Ray Canal: Screening water diversions protect fish and provide reliable sources of clean water for multiple uses.*

# Durham Dam Removal

*Restoring Fish Passage to Toppenish Creek and tributaries*

The Durham Dam Removal and Fish Passage project in eastern Washington State enhanced over 114 miles of critical stream habitat by removing a hydraulic barrier. The native aquatic species benefitted include the threatened Mid-Columbia steelhead (Oncorhynchus mykiss), as well as Pacific lamprey (Lampetra tridentata). In addition to the dam removal, the project installed downstream large woody material and a roughened channel to provide cover and stabilize the downstream channel. Project partners include the Yakama Nation and multiple landowners and managers. Removing the dam was a key action in the Yakama Nation's continuing effort to restore the Toppenish Creek Watershed located within the Yakama Nation Reservation boundaries. Both the watershed and the creek's native fish species are vital cultural resources of the Yakama Nation People.

*Completed Durham Dam removal project.*

*More than 114 miles of critical stream habitat are now available to native fish*

*Durham Dam removal project during construction.*

*Durham Dam prior removal: A concrete water control structure was built in Toppenish Creek in the early 1900s to control flow and divert water from the creek for irrigation.*

# Community Partners
## Restoring Native Fish Populations

## The Waihee Stream Fish Passage Project
## Oahu Island, Hawaii

The Waihee Stream Fish Passage Project on Oahu Island, Hawaii restored migratory native fish passage to over a mile of high-quality stream habitat. The native aquatic species benefitted include the unique Hawaiian stream gobies: Oopu nakea (Awous stamineus), as well as the Hawaiian freshwater shrimp: Opae kalaole (Atyoida bisulcata). A massive concrete water control structure built in 1935 and abandoned in the 1970s blocked fish passage, but completion of this project includes additional components added to the structure called "concrete rubble masonry" or CRM designed to be ascended by native stream organisms. Leadership provided by the Waihee Ahupuaa* Initiative ensured that community members were integral to conceiving, planning, and implementing the project. (*In the Hawaiian language, ahupuaa refers to a unit of land management that roughly follows watershed boundaries.)

**This structure blocked access to almost 30% of the length of Waihee Stream**

*Volunteers, landowner representatives, and resource agency personnel prepare the Waihee site for construction of the fish passage structure. A massive concrete water control structure associated with a stream gage was built in Waihee Stream in 1935 to monitor stream flow. This gage site was abandoned in the late 1970s, and the large structure remained in place. Over time, the downstream edge of the structure was scoured to become a sharply overhanging slab of concrete that could not be negotiated by native fish and invertebrates.*

*This species of native migratory goby is called oopu nopili in Hawaiian and can ascend waterfalls. Inset show pelvic fins that are fused to form a suction cup.*

CRM rock wall

*The recently completed project features a "concrete-rubble-masonry" (CRM) rock wall designed to be ascended by native stream organisms and various repairs to the lower margins and sides of the structure. The newly created steep CRM face will continue to exclude non-native species that are present in the lower reaches of Waihee Stream.*

# Fish Crossing

USFWS

*Bridge renovation completed on December 2011.*

## Stream Crossing Renovation at Watson Creek, Southeastern, Oklahoma

A fish passage project was recently completed on Watson Creek, a tributary to the Little River in southeastern Oklahoma. The project was completed with cooperation from John Hancock Forest Industries, the US Forest Service and Oklahoma Department of Wildlife Conservation. The Watson Creek project is part of a larger effort within the Little River drainage to restore the natural function of this river, where fish and other aquatic species can utilize all stream segments and still allow for the responsible harvest of timber in the area.

Watson Creek is a tributary to the Little River and is essential habitat for the Leopard darter (Percina pantherina) and the Ouachita shiner (Lythrurus snelsoni). The low-water crossing was completed in December 2011, and the embedded culvert structure was replaced with a box culvert structure. Vehicular traffic continues at this site.

*Before bridge reconstruction (August 2007).*

# Rio Paguate
## *Stream crossing renovation on Pueblo of Laguna, NM*

The New Mexico FWCO partnered with the Pueblo of Laguna to renovate two low-water stream crossings on the Rio Paquate. The Rio Paquate renovation is part of a larger effort to potentially restore Rio Grande cutthroat trout (Oncorhynchus clarki virginalis) to historically inhabited streams in the Rio Grande drainage. The low-water stream crossing renovations decreased disturbance to the stream, improved the ability of Pueblo of Laguna members to access renovation sites, and increased partnership between New Mexico FWCO and New Mexico tribal nations. USFWS staff worked closely with Pueblo of Laguna members to design and construct the project, and to monitor fish movement through the renovated stream crossing. The low-water stream crossing was completed in 2009, but suffered damage from a large flood in 2010. The low-water stream crossings were repaired in 2011 and 2012 and new methods used to protect them from future floods.

*Construction of low water stream crossing (2009).*

*Completed (repaired) low water stream crossing (2012).*

> Project SHARE would not have achieved its level of success in completing 125+ stream connectivity restoration projects without the committed capacity of stakehold member groups like the USFWS. Be it the funding capacity of the Fish Passage Program or the technical assistance offered by the Maine FWCO and Gulf of Maine Program, the USFWS is an active part of SHARE's habitat restoration team. Without the USFWS priority focus on fish passage, our program would not be where it is today.
>
> -Steven Koenig, Project SHARE Maine

# Fish way

*The Mequon-Thiensville Fishway, on the Milwaukee River in Thiensville Village Park provides fish passage and is a great educational opportunity*

© Stantee Aerial

## Reconnecting historic high-quality habitat on the Milwaukee River

The Mequon-Thiensville Fishway, on the Milwaukee River in Thiensville Village Park, was constructed to allow migratory fish to pass the Mequon-Thiensville Dam and reach historic, high quality spawning and rearing habitats. The 800 foot long fishway was made possible by a collaborative effort between Ozaukee County Planning and Parks Department, the Village of Thiensville, the City of Mequon, U.S. Fish and Wildlife Service, Wisconsin Department of Natural Resources (WDNR), and Marquette University. Funding for the project was provided by a National Oceanic and Atmospheric Administration (NOAA) American Recovery and Reinvestment Act (ARRA) grant to Ozaukee County, grants from the U.S. Fish and Wildlife Service, Wisconsin Coastal Management Program, and WDNR, and funding from the City of Mequon and Village of Thiensville. Fish are tracked in the fishway through a combination of electrofishing, an underwater camera, and passive integrated transponder (PIT) tags implanted in fish by the Ozaukee County Planning and Parks Department - Fish Passage Program and partners.

Since June of 2011, thousands of fish representing 31 different species have been identified passing through the fishway.

The fishway camera is accessible to the public thanks to funding from the NOAA/ARRA grant. Visit www.ozaukeefishway.org to view the live video feed and learn more about the Program.

Ozaukee Fish Passage Program

3/19/2012 09:52 33.606 PM (GMT-5.00)

*Fishway camera snapshot of northern pike.*

# Bringing Possibilities to Light

*Working Together to Help Restore Fish Passage
in the Red River of the North*

Christine and Hickson dams, located approximately 13 miles apart on the Red River near Fargo, North Dakota, have long been barriers to the migration of lake sturgeon, channel catfish, walleye, and other native fish species. Overcoming a host of obstacles to modify the two dams for fish passage, the City of Fargo worked closely with the Minnesota Department of Natural Resources, Midwest and Prairie regions of the U.S. Fish & Wildlife Service, North Dakota State Water Commission, North Dakota Game and Fish Department, River Keepers, and the Buffalo and Southeast Cass Watershed districts.

The NFPP, along with the Partners for Fish and Wildlife and National Fish Habitat Partnership programs, helped secure funding for construction, which began in November 2011. The two dam modifications were completed by February 2012 and consisted of installation of a rock arch rapids immediately below each of the dams. These actions improved access to needed spawning, rearing, and overwintering habitats on the Red River mainstem and its tributaries.

*Rock arch rapids: Christine and Hickson rapids now reconnect 68 upstream miles of the Red River and two headwater tributaries – the Otter Tail and Bois de Sioux rivers.*

*These rapids allow fish to freely move over 314 miles of the Red River before emptying into Lake Winnipeg, Canada.*

*Hickson Dam before.*

*A celebration was held August 29, 2012 at the Hickson Rapids site to commemorate fish passage at both dams. As part of the celebration, the Genoa National Fish Hatchery, with help from local high school students and AmeriCorps-Iowa members, released lake sturgeon fingerlings into the Red River below Hickson Rapids.*

# Two Dams Removed In Two Days

*Troy Dam #1 after removal*

*Dynamo Dam after removal*

Heavy equipment operators from US-FWS, removed two barriers to aquatic organism passage in the piedmont of North Carolina in two days. The Little River is a tributary to the Pee Dee River with 12 mussel species within the project area in imperiled status. This project marked the first for the Southeast Region as USFWS staff from Fisheries, Partners for Fish and Wildlife, Ecological Services, and National Wildlife Refuges (Refuges) led all phases of the barrier disposal, working hand-in-hand with American Rivers, local government and private landowners.

This area of the Little River historically supported American shad, blueback herring and American eel. Partners for Fish and Wildlife and Ecological Services staff completed the basic evaluation for both barrier removals, completed the restoration vision, and worked through the permitting process for the barrier owners. Students, volunteers, and Progress Energy assisted in fish and mussel surveys. Heavy equipment operators from Fisheries and Refuges completed the construction planning while working closely with Hertz's local heavy equipment rental company, and then managed

to remove the two structures in just two days, including having delivering and moving the equipment between the two sites. This was aided through the cooperation of the NC Department of Transportation to assist with traffic control.

## Troy Dam #1

*Troy Dam #1 was removed the following morning. A concrete structure built in 1940/1950's for the town's water supply no longer served its purpose. The project established a working relationship with the Town of Troy which is critical to the future removal of Troy Dam #2.*

## Dynamo Dam #1

*Dynamo Dam was the first barrier to be removed. This partially breached barrier was constructed for power generation in 1902 and stretched 157' across. Its removal re-opened 33.5 miles of main stem river and 83 perennial stream miles.*

These two barrier removals have opened a cost effective approach to removing small concrete structures by utilizing USFWS's highly skilled heavy equipment operators. Two additional dams are scheduled for removal in 2013 using this approach, at a significant savings.

# Restoring America's Greatest River

Since 2001, the Lower Mississippi River Fish and Wildlife Conservation Office has collaborated with the Lower Mississippi River Conservation Committee (LMRCC), the U.S. Army Corps of Engineers, and other partners to identify, prioritize and construct dike notches along the Lower Mississippi River. These projects provide fish passage, increase recreational opportunities, support nature-based tourism, support environmental education programs, provide habitat for bird species utilizing the Mississippi Flyway, restore and improve habitat for endangered pallid sturgeon, and promote multi-use management of the Lower Mississippi River.

Island 70 is located on the east bank of the Mississippi River in Bolivar County, MS about one half mile south of River Mile 610. The U. S. Army Corps of Engineers Vicksburg District constructed timber pile dikes within the Island 70 secondary channel in the 1960s to maintain the commercial navigation channel. Quarried stone was subsequently used to fill these dikes in the 1970s, converting them to low-maintenance, impermeable structures.

In 2010, the U.S. Fish and Wildlife Service partnered with LMRCC, U. S. Army Corps of Engineers Vicksburg District, and Wildlife Mississippi to develop a plan to restore flow through the 3.5-mile-long channel at Island 70. The two environmental goals of this project are to improve aquatic habitat in the channel by reintroducing a controlled amount of flow and to provide access to habitat for riverine fishes and other aquatic organisms. Equipment was used to construct notches in the dikes. More than 46,000 tons of stone were removed

*Pool habitat created from Dike 2 notch at Island 70.*

from the dikes during construction of these notches.

The Island 70 secondary channel rehabilitation project was completed in October 2011 at a cost of $150,500. Studies are underway with Lower Mississippi River Fish and Wildlife Conservation Office and Mississippi Department of Wildlife, Fisheries and Parks to evaluate the use of the secondary channels by riverine fishes. This project and others similar projects are part of the LMRCC's "Restoring America's Greatest River Plan," which is a landscape-scale conservation plan to improve the environmental health of the 954 river miles of the Lower Mississippi River. This project improve recreational and commercial fisheries, restore / delist threatened and endangered species, and promote economic development along the Lower Mississippi River.

*Notching Dike at Island 70.*

*Pilot Channel at Island 70 to reconnect secondary channels.*

# Free-Flowing Rivers

© Mark Miller photography

## *Kayakers Run South River Waynesboro, VA*

Kayakers can run the river past the old stacked stone Ramworks Dam in Waynesboro, VA now that the Appalachian Partnership Coordination Office has taken the 10 foot-high dam out of this river. Keith McGilvray, a Service biologist reported that brook trout and American

eel access 27 miles of coldwater nursery and spawning habitat upstream, important outcomes for partners that included Trout Unlimited and the Virginia Department of Game and Inland Fisheries. The dam was located on the South River, a Shenandoah River tributary.

*"Many fish passage issues within the contentious Klamath Basin are located at diversion points for agricultural use. Agriculture is the primary economy within the inland communities of the Klamath Basin while fisheries economies are important to the coastal communities of the Klamath Basin. While agriculture seeks to improve conditions for fish, many individual or cooperative agricultural operations do not have the financial or technical resources to correct their diversion points to meet fish passage criteria. Funds from the National Fish Passage Program are used to resolve critical fish passage issues but also protect the agricultural economy."*

**-Gary Black Local Farmer in the upper Klamath Basin, California; Fish Passage Contractor and Project Manager, Montague Water Conservation District**

# People and Endangered Species

William Hartley / USFWS

*Endangered Atlantic salmon*

## *Sweating for the Benefit of Fish and People: Downeast Rivers in Maine – Project SHARE*

Endangered Atlantic salmon in the Narraguagus, Machias, East Machias, and Pleasant rivers in Downeast Maine have access to an additional 114 miles of stream habitat after the Maine Fish and Wildlife Conservation Office, partners, interns, and volunteers decommissioned two roads, removed three log drive dams, and retrofit a bridge and four culverts. Work was sometimes done by hand in the water with nothing more than tools, hard work, waders and boots. Staff also completed 35 fish and habitat surveys in the upper Narraguagus River watershed.

USFWS

*Fish passage work that benefits Atlantic salmon, brook trout, river herring and American eel also comes with a socioeconomic benefit estimated at $ 57M*

# Reconnecting
# The Upper Colorado River Basin

## Hartland
### *Diversion Dam Modification*

Hartland Diversion Dam was an extreme safety hazard to boaters, especially for downstream passage. Addressing safety issues associated with the original dam provided fish passage as well as a corridor for boaters and increased safe public access on the Gunnison River. This project served to benefit local residents, visiting public, and commercial outfitters. Modifications to the dam provided fish passage and recreation while assuring the historic water rights of Hartland Irrigation Company.

*The dam renovation provides access to an additional 15 miles of habitat for native fishes in the Colorado River basin.*

The project was managed under the USDA, Resource Conservation and Development (RC&D) Program (local partnership council known as Painted Sky RC&D). Key stakeholders in the project along with ARRA and the US-FWS NFPP included the Colorado Water Conservation Board, Hartland Irrigation Company, Will Hutchins (private landowner), Walton Family Foundation, National Fish and Wildlife Foundation, Gunnison Basin Round Table, Colorado River Water Conservation District, Bureau of

Land Management, USDA-Natural Resources Conservation Service, Colorado Parks and Wildlife, Delta and Montrose Counties, Delta and Montrose Cities, Army Corp of Engineers, Bureau of Reclamation, The Nature Conservancy, Delta Conservation District, North Fork River Improvement Association and the Colorado Watershed Assembly.

Fragmentation of river reaches by dams and water diversion structures is one of the leading causes for the decline of native fishes in the Upper Colorado River Basin. The FWS considered the roundtail chub, flannelmouth sucker and bluehead sucker, as target species for the Hartland Dam renovation project. **This project (image above) assisted in restoring declining native fish populations and other aquatic resource populations and may help prevent a future need to list these three species under the ESA.** The three native fish species are in decline throughout their historical range and are listed as "species of concern" by most states in the Colorado River Basin.

*The Hartland Diversion Dam is located in Delta County on the Gunnison River in western Colorado. The 360 feet long, five-foot high dam and head gate structure is owned by the Hartland Irrigation Company and was constructed in 1881 for agricultural irrigation and stock-watering. Through the years, two widely known facts emerged that made the dam a prime candidate for modification. One was that fish of various species would congregate below the dam in an attempt to negotiate the dam and reach waters above. The second was that the existing structure was considered unsafe for downstream boat passage as evidenced by the death of several recreational boaters over the years.*

# The Science of Fish Passage

USFWS

## Research at Bozeman Fish Technology Center

In 2012, a project began at the USFWS Bozeman Fish Technology Center (FTC) to study fish swimming capabilities under varying conditions related to design of fish passage projects. The project links science and conservation delivery by developing species specific data related to design and implementation of projects. Funding was provided by the National Fish Passage Program and the Plains-Prairie Potholes LCC.

Current research led by Mr. Kevin Kappenman (Fishery Research Biologist, Bozeman FTC), Dr. Matthew Blank (Research Engineer, Montana State University), and Dr. Thomas McMahon (Professor of Fisheries, Department of Ecology, Montana State University) focuses on developing scientifically valid information on swimming abilities of little-studied native fishes of the Great Northern and Plains and Prairie Potholes conservation landscapes. Studies are conducted at Bozeman FTC in recently acquired open-channel flume, swim chamber, and artificial stream research systems, where variables such as water velocity, temperature, and substrate can be controlled and manipulated, and fish swimming performance and behavior can be monitored. Results will have application in several areas, including assessment of potential fish barriers, design of fish passage ways, and population viability modeling of species experiencing changes in aquatic habitats.

Another objective of this interdisciplinary research program is to provide graduate and undergraduate students the opportunity to learn from professional engineers and biologists, and thereby gain a broader base of knowledge for more effective future participation in solving fishery and landscape conservation problems.

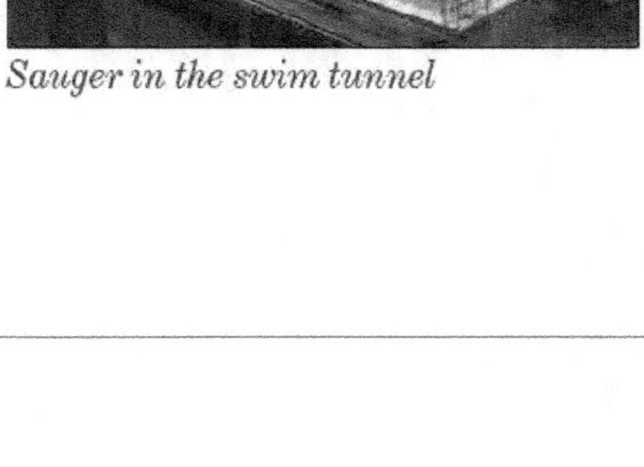

*Sauger in the swim tunnel*

*Graduate student David Dockery monitors the swimming performance of wild sauger in Bozeman FTC's open-channel flume.*

# A River of Life

*Juvenile salmonids schooling in Caswell Creek.*

Katrina Mueller / USFWS

## Caswell Creek Culvert Replacement Project, Matanuska-Susitna Borough, Alaska

Caswell Creek and its tributaries provide access to important spawning and rearing habitat for coho salmon and other salmonids. The project, pictured in the image below, consisted on replacing a known fish passage barrier on a tributary to Caswell Creek with a new culvert designed to maximize fish passage and accommodate flood flows.

BEFORE: *The original 60' culvert (middle) and two 36" overflow pipe system was a barrier to fish passage and did not adequately convey flood flows.*

AFTER: *A 13'x 9'X 100' embedded steel pipe arch culvert simulates natural stream conditions through the length of the culvert ,improved fish passage, and flood water management.*

# A New Migration Pathway for Coho Salmon

## Coyote Creek Fish Passage, Matanuska-Susitna Borough, Alaska

Coyote Creek is a tributary of the Little Susitna River. The Little Susitna River is the second largest coho salmon sport fishery in Alaska. Coyote Creek supports this fishery by providing important spawning and rearing habitat for coho salmon and resident fish species including Dolly Varden char and rainbow trout. Prior to restoration, the two culverts on the creek intersected Sunrise Road perpendicularly,while the creek was at a skewed angle to the road. This resulted in flow passing primarily through only one culvert, which was perched at its outlet. This design, combined with no flow conveyance through the second culvert, prevented of juvenile salmonid access to upstream rearing habitat. This project replaced the two undersized culverts with a much larger, fish-friendly culvert and also realigned the streambed. Stream banks adjacent to the new culvert were rehabilitated using bioengineering techniques.

AFTER: *The Alaska Fish Passage Program worked with partners to address the fish passage barrier by installing a 19 foot embedded box culvert designed to accommodate Coyote Creek's natural channel characteristics and provide a seamless connection between upstream and downstream habitat.*

By enhancing fish access to spawning, rearing, and over-wintering habitat, the Region 7 Fish Passage Program, in partnership with Alaska Department of Fish Game, Alaska Fish Habitat Partnerships and numerous private and local government landowners, is making important contributions to sustaining healthy populations of Pacific salmon and other anadromous fish species so important to Alaska's sport and commercial fishing economies and subsistence cultures.

BEFORE: *Two 4 foot culverts were causing an impediment to fish movement on Coyote Creek.*

# Restoring Stream Connectivity

*Whipple Ranch, Post-project.*

USFWS

## Fish Passage for Nevada's Endangered and Endemic Pahranagat Roundtail Chub

The National Fish Passage Program worked with partners and private landowners in Southern Nevada to restore connectivity and reconnect artificially separated populations of federally endangered Pahranagat roundtail chub. The Pahranagat roundtail chub occurs only in thermal waters in the Pahranagat Valley of southeastern Nevada. As the site was previously configured, water from the Pahranagat River seasonally passed through a culvert near the downstream end of occupied chub habitat and then dropped several feet into a drain. His-

toric surveys showed that both adult and juvenile chubs were carried downstream via this pathway and then were unable to return upstream where this population has historically persisted and bred. A series of low-gradient step pools were created downstream of the existing culvert, restoring upstream passage and ensuring increased survival and recruitment for this unique species. In addition to the step pools, a new removable flashboard weir was installed to replace the aging gate structure that regulated flow to the drain.

*Whipple Ranch, Pre-project.*

# Across
## San Antonio Creek...

The Ojai Valley Trail crosses San Antonio Creek near the confluence with the Ventura River and is an important transit corridor for Ventura County residents. The crossing formerly presented a significant barrier to endangered Southern California steelhead and threatened California red-legged frogs. Equally important, the site routinely filled with sediment requiring substantial and expensive maintenance while presenting a significant public safety hazard as the trail was frequently washed out for extended time periods. Between 2005 and 2011, the trail washed out three times and was closed for several months after each washout event. Damage and maintenance costs increased with each occurrence. Trail users often took serious risks by disregarding closed gates and warning signs to cross the channel and damaged trail while flows and debris were still present. Starting in November 2011, undersized culverts and a seasonal crossing were replaced with a modern and visually appealing bridge. The new bridge provides a safe year-round route for fish and humans as well as a scenic vantage point for users to view the natural beauty of the area.

*Looking south across San Antonio Creek.*

*This project provided access to fish and other aquatic species to over 10 miles of vital stream habitat*

*View of the southern approach to the crossing over San Antonio Creek which occurs at the confluence with the Ventura River.*

Mary Root \ USFWS

*Connecting 2 of the 60' truss sections.*

USFWS

# Geospatial Fisheries Information Network

## A Tool for supporting Aquatic Resource Conservation

**More than a Map!**

The Geospatial Fisheries Information Network - GeoFIN (previously known as the Fish Passage Decision Support System) is a web-based application developed by USFWS to address stream fragmentation and fisheries conservation. GeoFIN provides to the Service, its partners and the general conservation community a robust, yet easy to use, platform with advance tools for data analysis and easy access to a wide range of information including a comprehensive data set of dams (fish barriers) and other in-stream structures. These barriers prevent the natural movement of fish and other aquatic organisms and are considered one of the leading causes for the decline of fisheries resources nationwide.

The newly redesigned application contains web-GIS technologies and relational databases for delivering a much richer, advanced interactive platform for disseminating, visualizing, exploring data relationships and analyzing large volume of complex fisheries information. In addition to fish barriers layers, GeoFIN offers immediate access to a wide range of high-quality information from multiple sources using CLOUD computing and the latest on-line network and web technology. This means having instant access to a wide range of high quality information at your fingertips and ready for use at any moment using only your web browser.

As a communication tool, GeoFIN acts as a catalyst to engage others. It provides a powerful mechanism to create awareness and promote fisheries conservation actions by demonstrating needs and accomplishments. The new multi-dimensional architecture of GeoFIN offers the flexibility and scalability required to cope with the increasing demand of geospatial capabilities and expand its framework to support a wider range conservation actions.

*GeoFIN is a science-driven approach for making efficient, transparent decisions about where and how to expend resources for the maximum benefit of aquatic species.*

*Culverts are an example of frequently barriers to fish migration. Low water levels or elevated outflows ("perched") are common barriers to fish passage.*

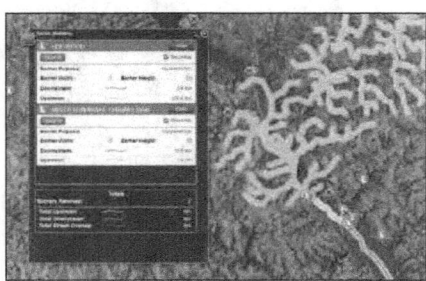

**Barrier removal simulation:** *This tool allows the user to perform a stream network analysis and visualize the potential streams impacted by the removal of a single or multiple barriers. The output includes a spatial visual representation of the stream reach impacted and numbers of stream miles upstream and downstream from the removed barriers. Future output will also include a list of fish species potentially impacted by removals.*

*Accomplishments: New widget showing a profile for FWS fish passage completed project.*

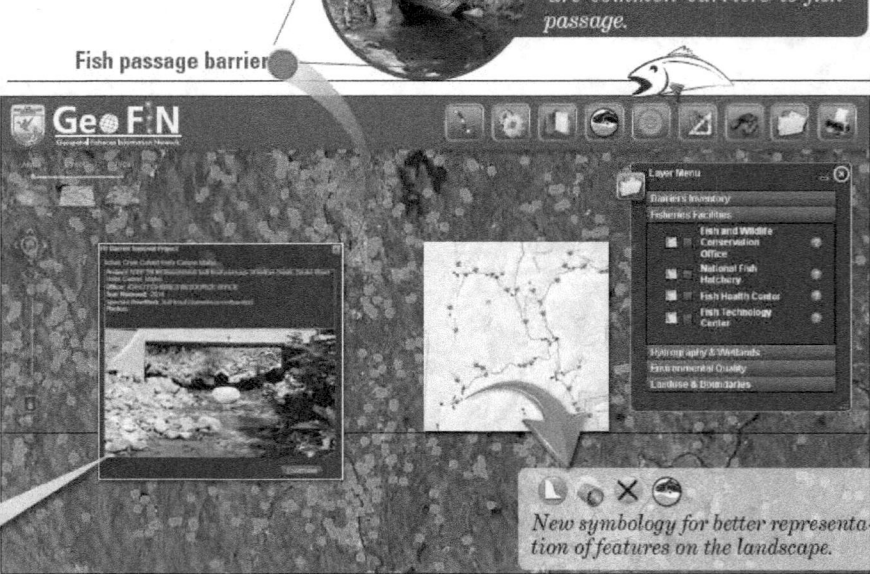

Fish passage barrier

*New symbology for better representation of features on the landscape.*

*GeoFIN virtual-GIS platform: This web-based platform allows users to explore and analyze data holistically and at multiple scales, from national to regional to a project level.* **Please visit us on the web at http://ecos.fws.gov/geofin/**

# National Fish Passage Program

## *Where are we going in 2013?*

### Increasing Awareness – Getting Our Story Out

- Expand the use of social media to include regular updates on Facebook and Twitter.

- Enhance support and collaboration through strategic briefings with key staff in and out of the Service.

- Program leadership to brief national partners in Washington, DC.

- Field staff to brief Congressional representatives in District Offices and conduct field site visits

- Provide national recognition to key partners and USFWS field staff involved in the program.

- Demonstrate social relevance of the program by linking resource outcomes with socioeconomic benefits.

### Enhancing Professional and Technical Capacity

- Develop a training plan to expand in-house technical capacity for aquatic habitat restoration using the stream restoration and fish passage training needs assessment.

- Promote the cost-benefit and human health and safety advantages of implementing improved fish passage standards for culvert projects throughout the States.

- Develop interagency USFWS flood disaster expertise team.

- Increase participation of on-the-ground implementation of fish passage projects through such avenues as USFWS heavy equipment operators and engineers.

- Work with federal agencies and NGOs to develop and administer road stream crossing infrastructure training for local communities and states.

- Support the development of water diversion engineers and expertise.

### Increasing Program Resources and Outcomes

- Regional and national funding opportunities showed the need that exists to restore fish passage and has demonstrated that the NFPP could effectively utilize resource increases. It is the goal to double its resources by 2016, which will involve working with partners and across government to better leverage existing funds.

- Fisheries personnel have identified more than 350 shovel-ready fish passage projects which have a combined funding need of more than $31.5M. We will continue to work towards addressing these projects and identifying others.

- Work with Hurricane Sandy recovery efforts to create and build flood resiliency within communities.

- Increase collaboration, efficiency, and effectiveness with key partners and across government by working together to assess and address factors that limit or hinder cooperation and collaboration.

- Expand collaboration with Landscape Conservation Cooperatives and other Service and federal government programs to maximize fish passage resources and resource benefits.

- Explore creation of cross-program and cross-agency "strike teams" to facilitate rapid emergency and recovery response after natural disasters.

- Develop a long-term approach to aquatic disasters by working with FEMA and others to build disaster resistant communities

- Removal of Veazie dam on the Penobscot River is slated for summer of 2013.

## A Plan for the Future

We will build on past success; capitalize on in-house engineering and technical capacity; and lead the way to improved science, increase on-the-ground results, work across landscapes and with communities, and ecological benefits for our nation's waterways, fish, and the American public.

## Regional Coordinators

Dan Shively
Fish Passage and Habitat Partnerships Coordinator
Region 1
Portland, OR
Contact: dan_shively@fws.gov

Sarah Conn / Jennifer FowlerPropst
Region 2
Albuquerque, NM
Contact: sarah_conn@fws.gov /
jennifer_fowlerpropst@fws.gov

Brian Elkington
Deputy Program Supervisor
Region 3
Minneapolis, MN
Contact: brian_elkington@fws.gov

Walter "Tripp" Boltin
Fish Biologist
Region 4
Atlanta, GA
Contact: walter_boltin@fws.gov

Janice Rowan
Senior Fish Biologist
Region 5
Hadley, MA
Contact: jan_rowan@fws.gov

Scott Roth
Fish and Wildlife Biologist
Region 6
Denver, CO
Contact: scott_roth@fws.gov

David Wigglesworth
Region 7
Anchorage, AK
Contact: david_wigglesworth@fws.gov

Donald Ratcliff
Fishery Biologist, Habitat Restoration Coordinator
Region 8
Stockton, CA
Contact: donald_ratcliff@fws.gov

## Fish Passage Engineers

Curt Orvis
Regional Fish Passage & Water Resources Team Leader
Region 5
Hadley, MA
Contact: curtis_orvis@fws.gov

Brian Waz
Hydraulic Engineer
Region 5
Hadley, MA
Contact: brian_waz@fws.gov

Brett Towler
Regional Fish Passage Engineer
Region 5
Hadley, MA
Contact: brett_towler@fws.gov

Bryan Sojkowski
Fish Passage Engineer
Region 5
Hadley, MA
Contact: bryan_sojkowski@fws.gov

Jesus Morales
Fish Passage Engineer
Region 5
Hadley, MA
Contact: Jesus_Morales@fws.gov

Wayne Stancill
Hydraulic Engineer - Fish Passage
Region 6
Pierre, SD
Contact: wayne_stancill@fws.gov

Bill Rice
Hydrologist
Region 7
Anchorage, AK
Contact: william_rice@fws.gov

## Headquarters, Washington, DC Office Support

Susan Wells
National Fish Passage Program Coordinator
Arlington, VA
Contact: susan_wells@fws.gov

José C. Barrios
Fish Biologist
Arlington, VA
Contact: jose_barrios@fws.gov

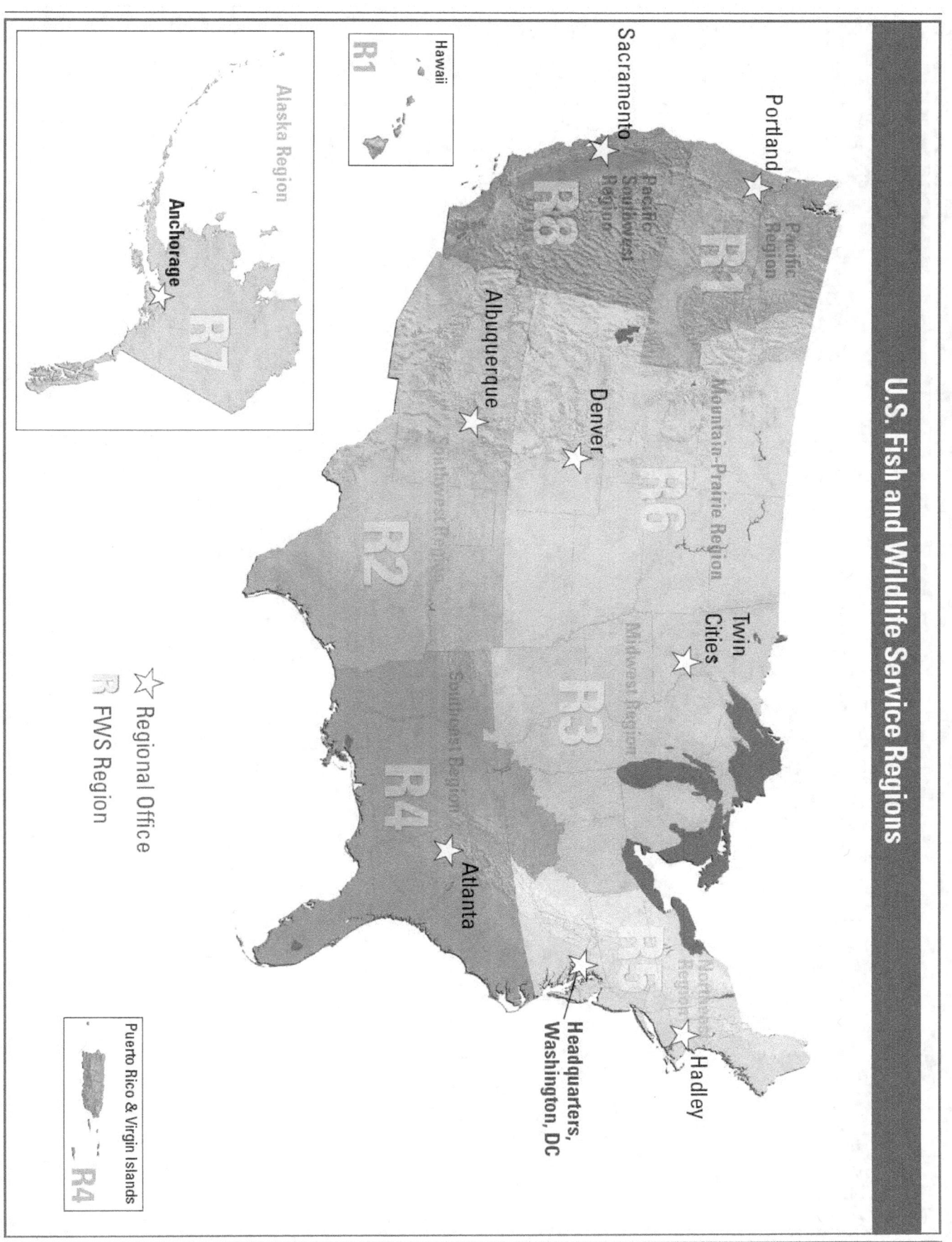

## U.S. Fish and Wildlife Service Regions

Portland

Sacramento

Pacific Region
R1

Pacific Southwest Region
R8

Albuquerque

Mountain-Prairie Region
R6

Denver

Southwest Region
R2

Twin Cities

Midwest Region
R3

Atlanta

Southeast Region
R4

Headquarters, Washington, DC

Northeast Region
R5

Hadley

Hawaii
R1

Alaska Region

Anchorage
R7

☆ Regional Office

R  FWS Region

Puerto Rico & Virgin Islands
R4

U.S. Fish and Wildlife Service
National Fish Passage Program
4401 N. Fairfax Drive
Room 760E
Arlington, VA 22203

703/358 2523 office
703/358 2044 fax

www.fws.gov

May 2013

www.ingramcontent.com/pod-product-compliance
Lightning Source LLC
Chambersburg PA
CBHW081135280526
45787CB00007B/3093

* 9 7 8 1 5 0 7 7 7 1 4 4 0 *